BLUES OF THE SKY

BLUES
OF THE SKY

Interpreted from the
Original Hebrew Book of Psalms

DAVID ROSENBERG

A POET'S BIBLE

HARPER & ROW, PUBLISHERS
New York, Hagerstown, San Francisco, London

ACKNOWLEDGEMENTS

These psalms first appeared, some in different form, in two limited editions from Angel Hair Books: *Some Psalms* (1973) and *Blues of The Sky* (1974). A few appeared in *Exile* and *The Coldspring Journal*. "Psalm 90" was printed *hors commerce* as a broadside.

FIRST EDITION

ISBN: 0-06-067009-6

Library of Congress Catalog Card Number: 76-9991

Designed by Patricia Girvin Dunbar

Contents

BLUES OF THE SKY

Psalm 1

Happy the one
stepping lightly over
paper hearts of men

and out of the way
of mind-locked reality
the masks of sincerity

he steps from his place at the glib café
to find himself in the word
of the infinite

embracing it
in his mind
with his heart

parting his lips for it
lightly
day into night

transported like a tree
to a riverbank
sweet with fruit in time

his heart unselfish
whatever he does
ripens

while bitter men turn dry
blowing in the wind
like yesterday's paper

unable to stand
in the gathering
light

they fall
faded masks
in love's spotlight

burning hearts of paper
unhappily
locked in their own glare

but My Lord opens
his loving one
to breathe embracing air.

Psalm 6

Lord, I'm just a worm
don't point to me
in frozen anger

don't let me feel
I more than deserve
all your rage

but mercy, Lord, let me feel mercy
I'm weak, my spirit so dark
even my bones shiver

my shadow surrounds me—I'm shocked
how long, Lord, how long
till you return to shine your light

return to me dear Lord
bring back the light
that I can know you by

because those that are dead
have no thought of you
to make a song by

I'm tired of my groaning
my bed is flowing away
in the nights of tears

depression like a moth
eats from behind my face,
tiny motors of pain push me

get out of here all you
glad to see me so down
your every breath so greased with vanity

My Lord is listening so high
my heavy burden of life floats up
as a song to him

let all my enemies shiver
on the stage of their total self-consciousness
and all their careers ruined in one night.

Psalm 8

My Lord Most High
your name shines
on the page of the world

from behind the lights
covering the heavens—
my lips like infants

held to the breast
grow
to stun the darkest thoughts

when I look up
from the work of my fingers
I see the moon and stars

your hand set there
and I can barely think
what is a man

how did you spare a thought for him
care to remember
his line

descending through death
yet you let him rise
above himself, toward you

held by music of words . . .
you set his mind in power
to follow the work of your hand

laying the world at his feet
all that is nameable
all that changes through time

from canyons to the stars
to starfish
at bottom of the sea

all that moves blazing a path
in air or water
or deep space of imagination on paper

My Lord Most High
your name shines
on the page of the world.

Psalm 12

Help, My Lord
where's the man
who loves you

where's the child
with human truth
behind him

helping him walk—
he grows into a lie
with his neighbors around him

speaking from made-up hearts
he becomes an empty letter
his lips sealed

tongue dried up
in its coat of vanity
its web of pride

"our lips belong to us
do what we want
to rise in the world

we don't want to hear
anything higher"
"I'm called I appear

by the human voice
the conscious victim
I send words to lift

whoever's waiting
I release him from lips
swollen in authority"

these words are free
like released energy
without violence

finite matter
broken open
with the tenderness of dawn

these words were always yours
My Lord, you sent into the present
lifting us from the inhuman

you are behind us
with every step in the infinite
through the swollen crowd around us

living lies
in a chain of lips
holding their children.

Psalm 19

The universe unfolds
the vision within:
creation

stars and galaxies
the words and lines
inspired with a hand

day comes to us
with color and shape
and night listens

and what is heard
breaks through deep silence
of infinite space

the rays come to us
like words
come to everyone

human on earth
we are the subjects
of light

a community
as it hears
the right words

creating time
the space of the sky
the face of the nearest star

that beats like a heart
in the tent where it sleeps
near the earth every night

then rises above the horizon
growing in our awareness
of the embrace

of inspiration
we feel as we turn
toward the warmth

starting at the edge of the sky
to come over us
like a secret love we wait for

love we can't hide
our deepest self-image
from

nobody holds back that fire
or closes the door
of time

words My Lord writes shine
opening me
to witness myself

conscious and unconscious
complex mind
warmed in an inner lightness

that moves me
to the simple beat
of time

testimony
of one author
speaking through history's pages

commanding my attention
bathed in light
around me

clean perfect notes
hearts play
make us conscious

we become the audience
amazed we can feel
justice come over us

our minds become real
unfold
the universe within

silence becomes real
we hear
clear words

become the phrasing of senses
lines of thought
stanzas of feeling

more lovely than gold
all the gold in the world
melting to nothing in light

sweet flowing honey
the right words
in my mouth

warming your subject
as he listens
breaking through his reflection

his image in the mirror
what mind can understand the failure
waiting in itself

silent self-image
created in the dark alone
to hold

power over others!
but justice comes over us
like a feeling for words that are right

absolutely
a mirror is pushed away
like a necessary door

we're free to look at everything
every shape and color
light as words

opening the mind
from nightmares of social failure
desperate routines

we're inspired above
the surface parade
of men dressed up in power

we see the clear possibility
of life growing
to witness itself

let these words
of my mouth
be sound

the creations
of my heart
be light

so I can see myself
free of desperate symbols
mind-woven coverings

speechless fears
images hidden within
we are the subjects of light

opening to join you
vision itself
my constant creator.

Psalm 22

Lord, My Lord, you disappear
so far away
unpierced by my cry

my sigh of words
all day My Lord
unheard

murmur of groans at night
then silence
no response

while you rest
content
in the songs of Israel

in the trust of fathers
you delivered
who cried to you

they were brought home
warm and alive
and inspired

but I am a worm
sub-human
what men come to

with a hate of their own futures
despised
and cheered like a drunk

staggering across the street
they howl after him
like sick dogs

"Let the Lord he cried to
save him
since they were so in love"

you brought me through the womb
to the sweetness
at my mother's breasts

no sooner my child eyes
looked around
I was in your lap

you are My Lord
from the time my mother found
me inside

make yourself appear
I am surrounded
and no one near

a mad crowd
tightens a noose around me
the ring of warheads

pressing ravenous noses
the mad whispering of
gray technicians

the water of my life evaporates
my bones stick through the surface
my heart burns down like wax

melting into my stomach
my mouth dry as a clay cup
dug up in the yard

I've fallen into the mud
foaming dogs surround me
ghost men

pierce my hands and feet
my bones stare at me
in disbelief

men take my clothes
like judges
in selfish dreams

make yourself appear
My Lord show me
the power

to free my life from chains
of bitter command
from the mouths of ghost men

trained on my heart
like a city
save me from mindless

megaphones of hate
you've always heard me
from my human heart

allowed me to speak
in the air of your name
to men and women

all who know fear
of losing yourselves
in vacant cities

speak to him
Israel's children
sing with him

all seed of men
show your faces
amazed in love

he does not despise them
he has not disappeared
from the faces of earth

from the ground of the worm
or the ear of the victim
I will always repeat

this song of life
with my hand that is free
from men who need victims

may our hearts live forever!
and the furthest reaches of space
remember our conscious moment

inspiring light
like those disappeared from memory
returned to the planet's earth

everyone has to appear
at death's door
everyone falls to the ground

while his seed carries on
writing and speaking
to people still to come

who remember to sing
how generous My Lord appears
to those hearing.

Psalm 23

The Lord is my shepherd
and keeps me from wanting
what I can't have

lush green grass is set
around me and crystal water
to graze by

there I revive with my soul
find the way that love makes
for his name

and though I pass through cities of pain, through death's
                                              living shadow
I'm not afraid to touch
to know what I am

your shepherd's staff is always there
to keep me calm
in my body

you set a table before me
in the presence of my enemies
you give me grace to speak

to quiet them
to be full with humanness
to be warm in my soul's lightness

to feel contact every day
in my hand and in my belly
love coming down to me

in the air of your name, Lord
in your house
in my life.

Psalm 30

Ligh praises
to you who raised me
up

so my critics fall silent
from their death wishes
over me

Lord Most High
I called you
and I was made new

you pulled me back
from the cold lip of the grave
and I am alive

to sing to you
friends, play in his honor
band of steady hearts

his anger like death
passes in a moment
his love lasts forever

cry yourself to sleep
but when you awake
light is all around you

I thought I was experienced
nothing was going to shake me
I was serious as a mountain

Lord, you were with me and then
you were gone
I looked for your face in terror

my body was made of clay
My Lord, it is now
I call you

what good is my blood my tears
sinking in the mud
is mere dust singing

can it speak
these words on my tongue, Lord
help me

turn my heavy sighing into dance
unbutton my shirt and pants
and wrap me in your glow

so my heart can find its voice
through my lips to you
warm and alive

rising
above all bitterness
high praises.

Psalm 36

Inside my heart I hear
how arrogance talks
to himself without fear

hidden from eyes
he flatters himself
but we see him on the faces

of false faces and words
thinking—even asleep—
how to squeeze love out

from feelings from words
how to put wisdom on her back
then hold his miniature knowledge back

your love fills a man, Lord
with a kind of air
making him lighter

he rises in measure of your judgment
above the mountains of thought
above the clouds of feeling

the strength of his measure stays
in the eyes returning to mountains
from the surface of the sea

he falls like any animal
standing up only by your mercy
his children grow in the shadow of your wings

feast on gourmet fare in your house
with water that sparkles from wells
beyond the reach of a mind

the fountain of life
is lit
by your light

you extend your embrace
to those who feel you are there
keep holding the loving

keep us from being crushed
by arrogant feet
by the hand of pride

the powerful are falling over themselves
their minds have pulled them down
there they will lie, flung down.

Psalm 49

Now hear this, world
all who live in air
important, ordinary, poor

my lips are moved by a saying
my heart whispers
in sound sense

I measure with my ear
this dark message and it opens
around my lyre

why should I make fear
dog my steps
growl in my thoughts

when the masters of vanity
breed in public for attention
rolling in scraps of money

no man can build a way
to God outside his body
to buy his continual release

to pay a ransom in every moment
for the gift of living
the price higher than his power to think

so that he could live forever
blind to his own falling
into the pit of death

but we all can see
the wisest man dies
along with the cunningly petty

their fortunes pass like mumbled words
among others
above their graves

it is there in hardened silence
the inheritors will join them
their bodily measure of earth

and though they put their names
on spaces of land,
their inward thoughts like words,

the mouths wither around them—
prosperous men
lose their intelligence

remember that in its saying
like animals who leave nothing to quote
those men pass on totally self-centered

like sheep gathered into the earth
their followers headlong after them
death's herd

their flesh stripped in death's store
and the big show made standing upright
erased in the sunrise

but My Lord holds the ransom
for death's vain embrace
as this music holds me—inside

don't be afraid of the big man
who builds a house that seems to grow
to the pride of his family

nothing will lie between
his body with its pride
and the ground he falls to

the life he made happy for himself
"so men may praise you
in your prosperity"

will find the company
of his fathers
around him as total darkness

his inward thoughts like words
the mouth withers around—
prosperous men lose their intelligence.

Psalm 58

Can this be justice
this pen to hold
they that move my arm

to follow them—blind stars?
They think I have submitted
to the vicious decorum of fame?

O generation come from dust
O no: you steel yourselves
to write; your hands

weigh, like a primitive scale,
selfish desire unfulfilled . . .
strangers from the womb

no sooner born and here
than chasing after
impulsive wishes

for which they will lie, cheat, kill.
Cancerous cold desire
gnaws in their brain

as the doctor
the greatest virtuoso specialist
numbs their consciousness

cutting into the chest
exposing the vital organ
totally blind to the truth.

Lord, cramp their fingers
till the arms hang limp like sausage,
grind down to sand

the teeth of the power-hungry
and let their selves dissolve into it
like ebbing tide on a junk-strewn beach

and when they in profound bitterness
unsheathe the sharpened thought
cut it out of their brain, Love!

make them disappear like snails
slime of their bodies melting away
or like babies, cord cut in abortion

to be thrown out as discharge
eyes withered in the daylight
though they never looked at it.

And let the children of greed like weeds
be pulled from their homes
and their parents blown away like milkweed . . .

The loving man will be revived
by this revenge and step ashore
from the bloodlust of the self-righteous

so that every man can say
there is justice so deep
a loving man has cause to sing.

Psalm 73

M y Lord is open
to Israel, to all hearts
within hearing

but I turned and
almost fell   moved
by flattery spoken

through transparent shrouds
impressing me
with the power of imagery

and fame of the mind
loving to strut
in its mirror

with its unfelt body
smooth as a machine
without a care in the world

prosperous mouthpieces
in their material cars
of pride

and suits of status
covering up
crookedness

their eyes
are walls
for wish-images

their mouths big
cynical
megaphones

self-made gods
whose words envelop the heads of men
hiding their fears

they go through the world
in self-encasing roles
in which they will die

lowered in heavy caskets
they made themselves
out of words

but meanwhile they suck in
most people
draining their innocence

until everyone believes
God isn't there
no wonder these men prosper

they push through the world
their violence
makes them secure

it seemed I opened my heart
and hand
stupidly

every day had its torture
every morning
my nerves were exposed

I was tempted to hide
to kill the moment
with pride

instead I tried to know you
and keep your song alive
but my mind was useless

until my heart opened
the cosmic door
to a continual presence

that is you
lighting the future
above the highway

down which self-flattering men
travel in style
to prisons of mind-locked time

they have their pleasures
cruelly pursued
and you urge them

to their final reward
you let them rise on dead bodies
so they have to fall

like a bad dream
the moment you awake
they are gone forever

my mind was dry thought
my feelings drained
through dusty clay

I was blindly
eating through life
like a moth in wool

I was crude
too proud
to know you

yet continually with you
take my hand
in love

it sings with you
inspired advice
leading to your presence

what will I want
but continual inspiration
in the present with you

what else will I find
in the blues of the sky
but you

and me in you
where am I in what universe
without you

my body dies of exhaustion
but you are the mountain
lifting my open heart

higher than a mind can go
into the forever
into the future

men who hide in their hearts
have bitter minds
they will lose

those people become no one
leaving you for an ideology
for a material car

but I waited for you
I was open, My Lord
to find my song

I found you here
in music I continue
to hear

with each new breath
expanding
to give me space.

Psalm 82

My Lord is the judge
at the heart
in the infinite

speaking through time and space
to all gods
he let be

"instead of lips
smoothed by success
and appearances

defend your silent critic
locked in barred categories
his conscience

painfully opened
by vicious systems
release him

let him speak
break the grip
of the prosperous

whose things enclose them
from the lightness of knowledge
the openness of understanding

they build in darkness
burying justice
digging at the foundation

of earth and men
the orbit
of trust"

I was thinking
you too are gods
heads of nations

thoughts of My Lord
but you will disappear
like the spirit you silence

your heads fall
like great nations
in ruins

My Lord, open
their consciousness
to share your judgment

all nations are men
you hear
beyond categories.

Psalm 90

Lord, you are our home
in all time
from before the mountains rose

or even the sun
from before the universe
to after the universe

you are Lord forever
and we are home
in your flowing

you turn men into dust
and you ask them to return
children of men

for a thousand years
in your eyes
are a single day

yesterday
already passed
into today

a ship in the night
while we were present
in a human dream

submerged
in the flood of sleep
appearing in the morning

like new grass
growing into afternoon
cut down by evening

we are swept off our feet
in an unconscious wind
of war or nature

or eaten away
with anxiety
worried to death

worn-out swimmers
all dressed up
in the social whirl

you see our little disasters
secret lusts
broken open in the light

of your eyes
in the openness
penetrating our lives

every day melts away
before you
our years run away

into a sigh
at the end
of a story

over in another breath
seventy years
eighty—gone in a flash

and what was it?
a tinderbox of vanity
a show of pride

and we fly apart
in the empty mirror
in the spaces between stars

in the total explosion of galaxies
how can we know ourselves
in this human universe

without expanding
to the wonder that you are
infinite lightness

piercing my body
this door of fear
to open my heart

our minds are little stars
brief flares
darkness strips naked

move us to see your present
as we're moved to name each star
lighten our hearts with wonder

return
and forgive us
locking our unconscious

behind the door
and as if it isn't there
as if we forget we're there

we walk into space unawed
unknown to ourselves
years lost in thought

a thousand blind moments
teach us when morning comes
to be moved

to see ourselves rise
returning witnesses
from the deep unconscious

and for every day lost
we find a new day
revealing where we are

in the future and in the past
together again
this moment with you

made human for us
to see your work
in the open-eyed grace of children

the whole vision unlocked
from darkness
to the thrill of light

where our hands reach for another's
opening to life
in our heart's flow

the work of this hand
flowing open
to you and from you.

Psalm 101

The city of your love
sings through me
before you, My Lord

you hold my writing hand
that makes my living
creative act

won't you come to me?
I sit here in my house
with an open heart

no willful image
blocks the door,
I just won't see

the theatrics of personality
crowding
the openness you allow

this art that hurts
those with ears for only jewelry
they go far away

locked within themselves
their self-flattery
I've reduced to silence

their narrow eyes
inflated pride
blown away

I'm always looking
for your people
to share this space

the contact of imagination
inspired
by necessity

beyond the stage doors
of weak characters
cut off from real streets

no more precious actors
costumed in sound
to litter this town with clichés

every morning
I silence with your light
desperate images

they run away
from the city of your name
that calls an open heart.

Psalm 121

I look up and find a mountain
to know inside
then light appears

inspired from most high
My Lord, creator
of earth and sky

we shall not be moved
this power inside
never fell asleep

over Israel
My Lord is in the light
the atmosphere

the power that moves my hand
through the sunlight that doesn't melt me
and by the moonlight

that moves us inside
to be inspired
above burning pride

desire
which is the mountain of our life
held in his air

and by his hand
we're free
to be moved

we may come and go
from now
to forever.

Psalm 130

I am drowning
deep in myself, Lord
I'm crying

I'm calling you
hear this voice, Lord
find me in your ears

the mercy of your attention
as it looks through the shell
of my selfishness

if you see only
vain impulses
marking the body's surface

the lines in the face
then there is no one
who'd hold up his head

but you allow us forgiveness
allow a song
coming through us

to you
as I call to you
as I rely on these words

as I wait
for you
more certain than dawn

through the steady ticking till morning
wait, Israel
even when watches seem to stop

My Lord comes to me
in a rush of love
setting my heart free

into a bright sky
we are lightened
in the mercy of his attention.

Psalm 133

It's so good, the turn of a season
people living for a moment as equals
secure in the human family

as sweet as spring rain
making the beard silky
Aaron's beard

his robes sparkle
rich with heaven's simple jewels
like the crown of dew

on Lebanon's Mt. Hermon
shared equally on the hills
of Israel

where the Lord graces our eyes
fresh from reborn wonder
as if we'd live forever.

Psalm 137

Into the rivers of Babylon
we cried like babies, loud
unwilling to move

beyond the memory
the flowing blood
of you, Israel

to an orchestra of trees
we lent our harps
silently leaning

when the enemy shoved us
"asking" tender songs of Israel
under heavy chains

"give us songs of Israel!"
as if we could give our mouths
to a strange landlord . . .

If I forget thee
sweet Jerusalem
let my writing hand wither

my tongue freeze to ice
sealing up my voice
my mind numb as rock

if I forget
your kiss
Jerusalem on my lips . . .

My Lord
remembers you, Edomites
Jerusalem raped vivid as daylight

you who screamed to strip her
strip her naked
to the ground

O Lady Babylon
Babylon the destroyer
lucky man who holds you

who crushes you
who opens your mind
to wither instantly in air

who holds up your crying babies
as if to stun them
against solid rock.

Psalm 139

There's nothing in me, My Lord
that doesn't open to your eyes
you know me when I sit

you note when I arise
in the darkest closet of my thought
there is an open window of sunshine for you

you walk with me
lie down with me
at every move await me

at every pause
you know the words
my tongue will print in air

if I say yes
you have already nodded
no—and you have shaken your head

in any doubts I lose my way
I find your hand
on me

such knowledge so high
I can never reach with a mind
or hold any longer than a breath

to get away from you
I could let my imagination fly
but you would hold it in your sky

or I could sleep with the dead in the ground
but your fire from the depths
would awaken me

I could fly on gold ray of sun
from dawn in east
west to stars of night

and your hand
would point the way
and your right hand hold me steady

however close I pull the night around me
even at midnight
day strips me naked

in your tender sight
black and white
are one—all light

you who put me together
piece by piece in the womb
from light

that work shines
through the form of my skeleton
on my song of words

you watched as my back steadied
the still-soft fuselage of ribs
in primitive studio deep within

you saw me as putty
a life unfashioned
a plane at the bottom of the sea

and the great book of its life
this embryo will write
in a body you have sculpted

My Lord—your thoughts
high and precious
beyond logic like stars

or like grains of sand I try to count
I fall asleep and awake
on the beach of your making

My Lord—stop the breath
of men who live by blood
alone and lie to your face

who think they can hide
behind the same petty smile
they use to smear your name

My Lord—you hear me hate
back your haters
with total energy

concentrated
in one body
that is yours and mine

My Lord—look at me
to see my heart
test me—to find my mind

if any bitterness lives here
lead me out
into the selfless open.

On Translating the Psalms

The psalms of the Bible are almost invisible to readers of modern literature today, and most readers of the Bible are as out of touch with the sheer poetry of the psalms as with modern poetry itself. This book is a poet's attempt to re-speak the psalms, to rediscover their quality of spokenness in modern poetic terms. In a way these versions are an offspring of modern biblical scholarship, which has thrown new light on early Hebrew language.

The psalms first struck me as needing a new translation precisely because of the awkwardness with modern poetry shown by modern Bible translators. I was reading a traditional Hebrew edition of the psalms from my father's bookshelf. The accompanying English translations seemed so "off." I came across one which seemed to draw on an incredible sexual image all the way through. The imagery of snakes and snakecharmers and everything else was just right, but it wasn't coherent because the translators were unconscious of the poem's inner form and flow. The language was so conceptualized for the sake of rhetorical effect that the imagery seemed irrelevant. I was thinking of them as poems then, not psalms, and that's how I began.

One of the clearest insights I've had into the role of the modern poet followed my father's death. I'd sent my father my first psalm attempts, and later I found he'd shown them to his rabbi. At the funeral chapel the rabbi, standing in front of my father's open coffin, read one of my psalms for the eulogy. I had to listen to him read it over the loudspeakers on that literal level, as prayer, and that's how the audience heard it. I was feeling painfully sad at the time, but I could hear that he didn't catch my phrasing and that he ignored my lines, echoing the rhythm and syntax of the King James translation. My ear cringed when I heard it like that: the music flattened and the whole, as I'd interpreted it, unraveled. On the other hand it was a humbling experience because I realized the literal strength of the original as almost-disembodied liturgy. A living poet can rarely expect to hear his work like that, ancient and new in the same breath, while he himself is part of a rapt audience.

My own attempts were a constant surprise. It was almost as if something would take my hand or mind and give me the shape of the whole poem—a shape I got not only from looking at many different texts, but from sensing the ancient, utterly lost original behind them: "utterly" in the sense of spoken. The original psalms became clearer to me as liturgy when I explored other English versions and the impossibility of literally speaking them. The modern three-line stanza I was using echoed for me both the original parallelism of ancient poetry and the basically triadic construction of the blues, which in turn is derived from gospel spirituals, a form of American liturgy. As I thought of the latter, I recognized a similarity between the "stone-righteous" blues man and the psalmist: a resistance to superstition, cynicism, and self-righteousness, without the pretense of perfectly transcending them; a desire not to sound smarter than one is, and to let one's heaviest feelings resonate in a gentle irony and become lightened in a harmonics of repetition. I had explored modes of this blues phrasing and stanza for years in my earlier work, beginning with what I'd learned from modern practitioners like William Carlos Williams.

There is an uncompromising spirit in the best modern poetry that confuses many people, and they conclude that the individualism of experimenting poets is a complete break with tradition. This conclusion is superficial because it ignores the element of vision. The best poets of any age reshape the mud of inertia into a hard clarity which may offend the squeamish. For instance, many people today may be shocked to discover how familiarly modern the absence of punctuation and conventional syntax is in the original psalms.

As the psalmist responded to a spiritual chord with the

direct speech of dialogue, the post-romantic poet has listened to speech patterns with the intensity of meditation. I worked toward a sense of wholeness for each individual psalm, using modern sources of imagery, stanza, line and rhythm, idiom and syntax. It was an experiment, and I explored earlier experiments in translation by poets from Philip Sidney and John Milton to Dante Rossetti. But these works were based on a Christian vision of the Old Testament, and, with the exception of Milton, these poets were in the dark about the almost-primitive originals.

I was led to Christian commentaries on the psalms, beginning with Saint Augustine's monumental work. Like Milton, I then turned to Jewish sources, to rabbinic commentary. Then to historical and textual studies—and here I became aware of modern scholarship and vast new sources in linguistic and archeological discoveries. I became involved in tracking the reconstruction of the original texts of the psalms, and even to the conjectured oral sources beyond. Modern psychological interpretations of the Old Testament, like those of Freud, Jung, and the sociologist Max Weber, tempered by inspired scholars like Buber, Heschel, and C. S. Lewis, helped me penetrate further into the past and its roots in our consciousness today. I tried to focus on the internal form of the psalms, their original lyric unity, and my versions attempt to break through to the original Hebrew and to parallel it, intuitively, in a modern form.

At first I was unsure of what to call these attempts because the religious idea of poetic inspiration is different from the traditional literary one. From a spiritual point of view, translation is a higher art than interpretation; from that point of view what's serious is what's literally spoken under the highest inspiration, as if it were the literal word dictated by the spirit—only the most inspired poet can translate it. The psalms, as they're read in the context of the Bible, are liturgical, the essence of literal language, almost a science of what is literal in spirit. So to call my work "interpretation" may seem to the orthodox mind to isolate it from a liturgical setting, from its reality of spirit.

I wanted to translate the form of the literal psalm, not the precise words, but the original atmosphere. Of course, there's no sure way to tell how I've succeeded or failed, and I'm content to consider them personal interpretations. Still, they are *attempts* at literal translation, from a sense of the lost ancient originals into the form of a psalm or hymn, a poem of "public meditation." I try for the atmosphere of completeness with the limited inspiration I can get from the tradition of modern secular poetry and its drive toward a literal expression of feeling, an immediacy of author's presence in the process of listening to himself speaking.

I didn't start with that grand an idea. I was just interested in how the psalms would sound as spoken poetry. I thought they would come out sounding very light in terms of unsophisticated ideas of coherence but odd, the way primitive works of art are, especially because I was attempting to focus on the early Hebrew as opposed to the Latin, Greek, or Masoretic Hebrew versions (although this traditional Hebrew text set down in medieval times is remarkable in its preservation of an already ancient poetics). The language of the later versions is more conceptualized than the originals. It is *there* that the density of imagery and inspired word-play is watered down; and the translations were not made by poets, who might be more sensitive to the strengths and weaknesses of the language they are translating *into*. It's a different story when you listen to poets. Even though Sidney and the Countess of Pembroke were working from the Latin, they were trying to establish a form, a formal whole, in the spirit of Renaissance exploration. They were experimenting in their own language, a relatively new language then, as Hebrew was for the psalmists.

Modern exploration by poets and artists has gone a long way toward reestablishing contact with primitive imagery. The ancient Hebrew poets built a "parallel" imagery that is similar to the modern texture of collage. It is not the kind of linear imagery in the Christian tradition of Western literature out of Greece and Rome. T. S. Eliot was applying collage to that tradition in "The Waste Land" more than a half-century ago. Parallel imagery comes up often in the psalms,

50

where a composite series of images creates, not a tapestry, but a psychological atmosphere of reality.

As Apollinaire, for example, applied it in his poetry, collage is an extension of the metaphor. It suggests the expansive feeling of an infinite range of combinations of images, mirroring the universe as we now tend to see it and as the psalmists first felt it. Their work conveys the strangeness but also the human response to the beauty of a universe beyond us: within, without. Poets have become free to explore the boundaries of poetic form as well as its metaphorical relationship to the boundaries of self, and I applied my experience to the integrity of each psalm. Just as we've begun to realize the scope a technique like collage opens to us, modern biblical scholarship has realized the vast range of subtleties behind the ancient technique of parallelism.

Although the original psalms are formally intricate, the speaking voice always penetrates the texture. Likewise, the flexibility of common speech in poetry today puts the spotlight on phrasing, especially since collage opened up the field of imagery. And in a way the process of becoming a poet involves listening for one's voice in the texture of phrasing. In fact it is often the texture of a pattern of phrasing that unifies a modern poem, and this is what makes it possible to identify today with the poetic context of a Hebrew psalm. As the psalmist discovers a higher plane in the faith of his own voice, the modern poet is also a discoverer, a listener, and no longer the romantic inventor from scratch he or she once seemed to be. The psychological situation of the poet struggling with himself (no longer calling on a Greek muse) parallels the psalmist's dialogue-struggle with his God—the faith in a higher order or music lifts the poem out of monologue. A truly original poem today is almost an act of faith itself as it moves toward discovering its own inclusive form.

As a poet, then, I'm both speaking and listening to myself speak. I recognize that I, personally, have nothing startlingly "new" to say. And so I become a transmitter, as was the original psalmist in his anonymity. He amplified a communal body of knowledge which very much did have something to say, going back to the oral tradition from which poetry comes; he was a translator into poetry, and that's where I find myself with the psalms today. The history of modern poetry records a disaffection with the classical traditions and a re-encounter with the primitive origins of society, an exploration of the roots of poetry itself, both psychologically and historically. Confronting the psalms in their literal context, one realizes how difficult it is to conceive of a universe for which poetry is a way to speak directly and openly. We have to create the context ourselves, in each poem, in which we can speak openly. And in that act is the tendency to overdraw our originality and obscure our calling.

In the psalms, the play is not in what's being said but in becoming aware of the total surrounding context—a kind of light irony that the parallel imagery reflects on human presence in a divine atmosphere. Sometimes I had to fight the impulse in my versions to use a line that sounded witty or heavily ironic. This consciousness of how we sound when we're *being* ironic made me keep in mind the example of lightness in the *Divine Comedy* as it explodes irony: every time one thinks the poet is being incredibly ironic, he goes a step further, until the atmosphere is lightened. And that atmosphere of self-conscious realism goes back to early Hebrew civilization—the feeling that one's purpose is to witness and not to be some theoretical or supernatural agent, that poetry is a feat of consciousness. Expanding one's consciousness doesn't mean violent life-change; it means continually adjusting oneself to an awareness of reality—to speak and to listen in concert, to lighten the burden of self-consciousness.

In modern poetry, I learned a sophisticated equivalent of the blues from the work of Gertrude Stein. She explored the psychological effects of repetition and demonstrated the spirit that links poetry, meditation, and liturgy. Her example shattered a fashionable cynicism, helping to establish the positive discipline of a head-on, self-effacing confrontation with the most serious qualities of lightness. The thoroughness of her experiments were also an inspiration for me to plunge deeper into biblical studies.

When I started to work on the psalms, I didn't want to go

52

too deeply into biblical research, I didn't want to wrestle with the broader context of authenticity. I was satisfied my versions were little translation experiments. My personal awareness of the psalms as liturgy overtook me while I was translating one that I thought was written in anger and which is usually translated as if it was. I suddenly realized it was not anger at all but an intense depression, a self-conscious awareness of failure. The psalmist was facing depression and not allowing himself to respond with bitterness. Instead, even as his voice speaks bitterly, he overcomes despair with his song's urge toward lightness. Its formal repetitiveness parallels the strength of his faith in a higher being whose ear he approaches as he listens to himself.

David Rosenberg

August, 1974
New York, New York